SAFE BY DESIGN
SAFETY
IN EXTREME CLIMATES

by Kaitlyn Duling

pogo

Ideas for Parents and Teachers

Pogo Books let children practice reading informational text while introducing them to nonfiction features such as headings, labels, sidebars, maps, and diagrams, as well as a table of contents, glossary, and index.

Carefully leveled text with a strong photo match offers early fluent readers the support they need to succeed.

Before Reading

• "Walk" through the book and point out the various nonfiction features. Ask the student what purpose each feature serves.

• Look at the glossary together. Read and discuss the words.

Read the Book

• Have the child read the book independently.

• Invite him or her to list questions that arise from reading.

After Reading

• Discuss the child's questions. Talk about how he or she might find answers to those questions.

• Prompt the child to think more. Ask: Have you ever been in a very hot place? What about a very cold place? What did you do to protect your body from the extreme temperatures?

Pogo Books are published by Jump!
5357 Penn Avenue South
Minneapolis, MN 55419
www.jumplibrary.com

Library of Congress Cataloging-in-Publication Data

Names: Duling, Kaitlyn, author.
Title: Safety in extreme climates / by Kaitlyn Duling.
Description: Minneapolis, MN: Jump!, Inc., [2020]
Series: Safe by design | Audience: Ages 7-10.
Includes bibliographical references and index.
Identifiers: LCCN 2018061515 (print)
LCCN 2019004687 (ebook)
ISBN 9781641288866 (ebook)
ISBN 9781641288842 (hardcover: alk. paper)
ISBN 9781641288859 (pbk: alk. paper)
Subjects: LCSH: Climatic extremes–Juvenile literature.
Extreme environments–Juvenile literature.
Technological innovations–Juvenile literature.
Classification: LCC QC981.8.C53 (ebook)
LCC QC981.8.C53 D85 2020 (print) | DDC 304.2/5–dc23
LC record available at https://lccn.loc.gov/2018061515

Editor: Susanne Bushman
Designer: Michelle Sonnek

Photo Credits: photo one/Shutterstock, cover (thermometer); Mykola Mazuryk/Shutterstock, cover (ground); Stacey Anna Alberts/Shutterstock, cover (sun); ANURAK PONGPATIMET/Shutterstock, 1; Yellow Cat/Shutterstock, 3 (hat and glasses); eurobanks/Shutterstock, 3 (water bottle); Bet_Noire/iStock, 3 (sunscreen); Nickolay Stanev/Shutterstock, 4; Volodymr Goinyk/Shutterstock, 5; Sergey Novikov/Shutterstock, 6-7; iroha/Shutterstock, 8-9; 06photo/Shutterstock, 10; blvdone/Shutterstock, 11; Korkusung/Shutterstock, 12-13; BanksPhotos/iStock, 14-15; bgblue/iStock, 16 (left); gst/Shutterstock, 16 (right); Suzanne Tucker/Shutterstock, 17; Steve Sparrow/Getty, 18-19; Shamleen/Shutterstock, 20-21; Palmer Kane LLC/Shutterstock, 23 (thermometer); TanyaRozhnovskaya/Shutterstock, 23 (scarf).

Printed in the United States of America at Corporate Graphics in North Mankato, Minnesota.

TABLE OF CONTENTS

CHAPTER 1

EXTREME TEMPERATURES

It is 134 degrees Fahrenheit (57 degrees Celsius)! Where are we? This is Death Valley in California. It is a desert.

Antarctica is the coldest place in the world. Temperatures here can be around –100°F (–73°C). How do people survive in these extreme **climates**?

Our bodies have an average body temperature. It is 98.6°F (37°C). We need to keep it safe from extreme heat and cold!

Layers **insulate** the body. Hats help keep body heat in. Almost 20 percent of body heat can be lost without them!

Frostbite is dangerous. It affects fingers and toes most often. Just 30 minutes spent in –10°F (–23.3°C) weather can cause frostbite. Yikes!

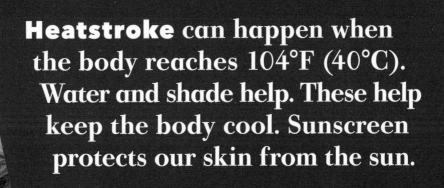

Heatstroke can happen when the body reaches 104°F (40°C). Water and shade help. These help keep the body cool. Sunscreen protects our skin from the sun.

DID YOU KNOW?

Some days, sunscreen is extra important! Why? The sun's rays can be stronger. Scientists can **predict** their strength.

CHAPTER 2
CITY SOLUTIONS

Think of a big city. There are tall buildings. Cars zoom by. Sidewalks are busy with people. A lot of **energy** is produced. The temperature rises. The city becomes a **heat island**.

It can be hard to stay cool in cities. Why? There isn't much shade. Once a city heats up, it keeps getting warmer. Extreme heat can cause a **heat wave**. Body temperatures rise. People and animals can get sick.

Urban planners help. How? They plan and design. Planting trees is one way. Trees provide shade. They **absorb** sunlight and heat.

Light-colored roofs and streets can help, too. These **reflect** more sunlight. They absorb much less heat.

DID YOU KNOW?

Some skyscrapers have gardens on their roofs! Why? The plants absorb heat and sunlight.

skywalk

Cities can get cold, too. Some have skywalks. These protect people from snow and **windchill**.

Engineers consider windchill when designing buildings. They must be insulated. They cannot let air in or out.

> **DID YOU KNOW?**
>
> Native Americans invented the igloo. It uses snow to insulate and protect against wind. Brr!

CHAPTER 3

CHANGING CLIMATES

Earth's temperature rises each year. This impacts extreme weather.

Climate change worsens storms and floods. Even snowstorms could get worse! A hotter planet can mean more **droughts**. To plan for water shortages, cities store water for later use. Some cities forbid watering grass.

DROUGHT
DO NOT
WATER GRASS

As the climate changes, we might see even more extreme temperatures. How can we help? We can use less electricity. We can plant more trees.

TAKE A LOOK!

Earth is heating up. How does climate change happen?

1. Gases are released when we use fuel.
2. The gases trap the sun's heat.
3. Trees and plants cannot absorb all of the energy.
4. Rising temperatures change the weather.

Hit the pool in the summer heat. Don't forget the sunscreen! Bundle up during winter storms. Do you have your hat? How do you stay safe in extreme weather?

ACTIVITIES & TOOLS

BUILD YOUR OWN BLUBBER

One of the things that keeps an animal warm in cold conditions is blubber. Polar bears, whales, and walruses all have layers of blubber. Make your very own blubber gloves and test them out.

What You Need:

- two one-quart plastic bags
- duct tape
- large bucket of ice water
- rubber gloves
- can of shortening
- foam packing peanuts
- cotton balls or feathers

1 **Fill one of the plastic bags about ¾ full of shortening.**

2 **Put on your gloves.**

3 **Insert one hand into an empty plastic bag and the other into the bag filled with shortening. This is your blubber bag.**

4 **Have an adult help you tape the bags closed around your wrists.**

5 **Put your covered hands into the tub of ice water. Which hand is colder?**

6 **Repeat this experiment with foam peanuts, cotton balls, feathers, or other materials in place of the shortening. Predict which will work best to keep your hand warm. Record your results.**

absorb: To take in or soak up.

climate change: A long-term shift in worldwide climate and weather, often attributed to an increase in global temperature due to the increased use of fossil fuels.

climates: Typical weather conditions in certain areas over long periods of time.

droughts: Periods of very little rainfall.

energy: Usable power.

engineers: People who design systems, structures, products, or machines.

frostbite: The freezing of skin and the tissue below due to exposure to extremely cold temperatures.

heat island: An urban area in which temperatures are significantly warmer than rural and surrounding areas.

heatstroke: A serious condition caused by extremely high body temperature that can cause collapse, unusual behavior, and unusual sweating.

heat wave: A long period of excessively hot weather, especially compared to the usual weather in the region.

insulate: To cover something with material to stop heat from escaping.

predict: To say what will happen in the future.

reflect: To throw back light, heat, or sound from a surface.

urban planners: People who design and develop cities and towns.

windchill: The degree to which the wind affects how cold the air feels.

INDEX

TO LEARN MORE

Finding more information is as easy as 1, 2, 3.

1 Go to www.factsurfer.com

2 Enter "safetyinextremeclimates" into the search box.

3 Choose your book to see a list of websites.

FACT SURFER